Exploring Plants

Michele S Long

This workbook and others are made possible
by a generous donation
from the Service League of Hickory
and the Rotary Club of Hickory.

Copyright © 2022 by Michele S Long

All rights reserved. No part of this book may be reproduced

without written permission from the author.

Contents

WARNING 1
OVERVIEW 3
    Activity – Take A Walk 3
    Tip – Identify That Plant 3
    Research – Your Favorite Plant 3
PLANTS 6
    Activity – Visit A Park 6
    Activity – Counting Plants & Animals 7
PLANT PARTS 9
    Activity – Plant Parts 11
  ROOTS 12
    Research – The Sweet Potato 12
    Activity – The Odd One Out 13
    Activity – Carrot Hunt 14
  STEMS 15
    Activity – Eat A Snack 15
    Activity – Edible Stems 16
    Tip – Learn to Love Vegetables 17
  LEAVES 18
    Activity – Evergreen Leaves 18
    Activity – Counting Leaves 19
    Activity – Leaf Tasting 19
    Activity – Sort Leaves 20
  FLOWERS 21
    Activity – Flowers Coloring Page 22
    Edible Flowers *23*
    Experiment – Edible Flower Popsicles 24
  FRUIT 25
    Activity – Name That Fruit 25
    Activity – Fruit Math 26
    Activity – Mr. Greene's Fruit Stand 27
  SEEDS 28

Activity – Look at Those Seeds 28
Experiment – See Your Seed Germinate 29
Experiment – Can Seeds Sprout Without Soil? 30
Activity – Plant Parts 32
Activity – Name That Part 33

PLANT TYPES 35

VASCULAR SYSTEM 36
POLLINATORS 37
MOSSES & WORTS 38
Mosses 38
Worts 38
Activity – Mosses & Worts 38
FERNS 39
GYMNOSPERMS 39
Activity – Gymnosperms 39
ANGIOSPERMS 40
Activity – Plant Types Crossword 41
Activity – How Seeds Travel 42

PLANT LIFE CYCLE TYPES 44

ANNUALS 44
Cool-Season Annuals 44
Warm-Season Annuals 44
The Rest (Half-Hardy) 45
Choosing Annuals 45
BIENNIALS 46
PERENNIALS 46
Temperennials 47
Choosing Perennials 47
Activity – Perennials 48

HOW PLANTS GROW 50

PLANT LIFE CYCLE 51
PLANT NEEDS 52
PLANT TAGS 53
Name 53

Description	53
Light	53
Full Sun	53
Part Sun	53
Full Shade	53
Water	55
Dry or Very Well-Drained	55
Normal or Well-Drained	55
Moist or Damp	55
Bloom Time	55
Spacing	55
Size	55
Shape	56
Zone	56
Care	56
Use	56
Wildlife	56
Attracts	56
Detracts	56
Planting Steps	56
Keep or Toss	56
Activity – Different Tags	57
Activity – Color Peony	58
HOW PLANTS EAT	**60**
Chlorophyll	62
Question – Do Plants Bleed?	62
WHERE PLANTS GROW	**65**

Zone	65
Research – Your Growing Zone	65
Native	66
Plants	*66*
Research – Native Plants	66
Soil	*66*
Cecil soil	67
Sandhill soil	67
Organic wetland soil	67
Research – Native Soil	67
HOW PLANTS MOVE	**69**
Activity – Pretend To Be A Flower	69
Activity – Recap Word Search	70
GLOSSARY	**72**
Research – Add Your Definitions	75
RESOURCES	**77**
Certificate of Completion	77
Citations	77
Answers	78
A NOTE FROM THE AUTHOR	**81**

Meet **Alejandro**

His name means "Warrior." The name fits him well as he is a fierce defender of pollinators - bees in particular.

Image of watermelon

Warning

Warning: Not all activities, experiments, field trips, questions, research, suggestions, and tips are appropriate for all children or in all situations. Implementation should be undertaken in appropriate settings and with appropriate parental or adult supervision.

OVERVIEW

Overview

When we think of living things, we usually think of plants and animals. Plants provide us with food, shelter, medicine, and so much more. Plants clean our air, boost our mood, and can help us focus better. Visiting a park filled with trees, grass, shrubs, and flowers may help us relax and feel better too.

Join us as we explore many different types of plants that we find in the world around us!

Activity – Take A Walk
Take a walk around your yard and count at least ten plants you think are beautiful. Take a picture of your favorite.

As you walk, notice the sounds around you. What do you hear?

Birds		

Tip – Identify That Plant
Use a free phone app like the one found at picturethisai.com to identify your favorite. Use the photo you took in the previous activity. What is the plant name?

_____

_____

Research – Your Favorite Plant
Name four beneficial characteristics of your favorite plant.

1	
2	
3	
4	

Image of teens planting

PLANTS

EXPLORING Plants

Plants

A plant is a living thing that generally grows in soil. Plants can be found almost everywhere globally except in very cold, very hot, very high, or very deep places. Animals would not have oxygen to breathe and little food without plants. Plants are an essential part of our world.

Examples of plants that we might see are trees, flowers, grass, and weeds. Parks are a great place to see many different types of plants.

Activity – Visit A Park

Visit a local park. Play a scavenger hunt game with the things you see at the park.

List four types of plants:

1	
2	
3	
4	

List four types of animals:

1	
2	
3	
4	

List four types of seeds:

1	
2	
3	
4	

What is your most exciting find?

_____

Activity – Counting Plants & Animals

Counting Plants & Animals
AN ADDITION GAME

Directions: Count how many of plants and animals you see. Write the answers in the box provided below.

Plants ☐   **Animals** ☐

There are twelve (12) plants and ten (10) animals.

PLANT PARTS

Plant Parts

The main parts of a plant are the roots, stem, leaves, flowers, fruit, and seeds. The bean plant's image below has all the main plant parts – roots, a stem, leaves, flowers, fruit (the bean pods), and seeds (the beans). The herb on the next page has leaves, stems, and roots.

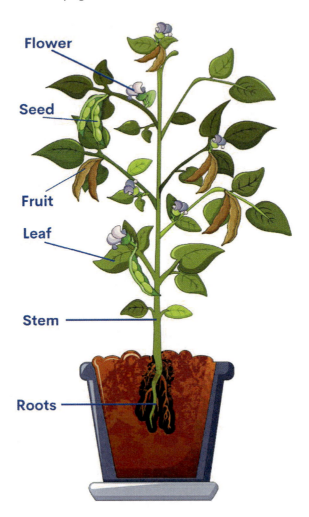

Image of a Bean Plant

Each plant part has an essential role in the plant's growth and health – the roots absorb nutrients and water, the stem supports the plant, the leaves make food using photosynthesis, and the flowers and fruit spread the plant's seeds. By learning what each part does, we can understand plants better and learn how to best care for them.

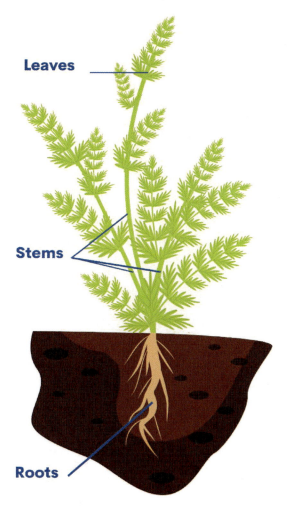

Image of an herb plant

Activity – Plant Parts

Plant Parts

Write the name for each part of the plant using the word list below.

root   flower   seeds   stem   fruit   leaves

Circle the correct answer for each question below.

Which of these items are edible leaves?
   a. carrot   b. potato   c. kale   d. tomato

Which of these items are edible roots?
   a. potato   b. kale   c. tomato   d. asparagus

Which of these items are edible stems?
   a. tomato   b. celery   c. carrot   d. potato

Which of these items are edible fruit?
   a. potato   b. kale   c. tomato   d. asparagus

Which of these items are edible seeds?
   a. acorn   b. pine cone   c. coconut   d. beans

Roots

Roots are the plant part that holds a plant in the ground and helps it get water and **nutrients** from the soil. Roots also store energy for the plant.

Some roots are **edible,** which means we can eat them. Some edible roots are carrots, potatoes, beets, and onions.

Some roots have a **taproot system** which means it has one main root with little, smaller roots. A carrot would be an excellent example of a taproot.

Some roots have a **fibrous system** which means it has many small roots. A tomato plant has a fibrous root system.

Sweet potatoes are an excellent example of roots that store energy for the plant.

Research – The Sweet Potato
The sweet potato is a nutrition-packed vegetable. List several benefits.

Help prevent cancer		

Activity – The Odd One Out

The Odd One Out

Cross Out The One That Is Not An Edible Root

Activity – Carrot Hunt

Help The Bunny Find His Favorite Root Vegetable

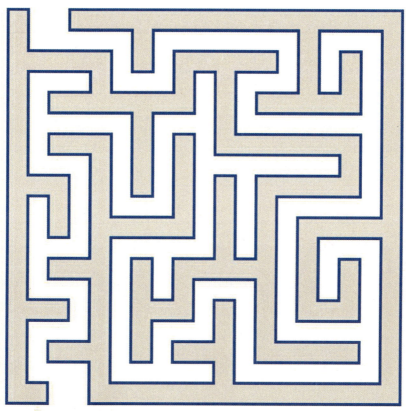

Stems

A stem is the plant part that holds the plant up and carries water and nutrients to the leaves. The stem also stores nutrients for the plant and creates new plant tissue – new smaller stems off the main stem where leaves and flowers grow.

Examples of edible stems include asparagus, celery, rhubarb, broccoli, and cauliflower.

Stems have **nodes** and **internodes**. Nodes are the part of the stem that branches off into smaller stems that hold leaves and flowers. Internodes are the central part of the stem between the nodes.

Activity – Eat A Snack
Celery is a healthy snack whether eaten by itself or with dip. Be creative in creating your yummy celery snack. Record your "recipe" below.

_____
_____
_____

Activity – Edible Stems

```
F D Y G F B U Z W H A X N H C G J D P W G V R B T O Z L E L
C O N E D Z L T N V G C O T M R B I H R Q D E N S T G V Y A
F H T B L P C J X U P E C U D C Y R V S N I H Y W F U L M P
R I L V U I R P V N H A A K S G Q W W I N Z R H U B A R B V
N I E D O G Q O N P P X U K C Y U M P E N Q F X Y K R S U D
L L E C B R T J F M J U L V Z V R Z I G L P X A G A Z R O I
W N K E H L B F Y L G J I T L S H I P Q Y I O I S S N D S F
M D L L M O R O L G R H F H Z S J C U S A U N E P H Y B O R
C V N E M T O I Q F S D L Q E V J Y D N A O L Z P O C W I W
H V M R Z U C R C F A H O T Z N Q A S P A R A G U S K L A S
G E Z Y D S C D D S W I W N F H N P F F M Q M L C J F B H W
S A D E R R O Q O Q J H E S Q S H A L L O T E T Y L E S F I
F Q S B L O L L Y F I V R R W Q L N Z G V A Q P W X X M Y S
B T G U T O I H R W R W D Z W K U C N X D J Z S K X N F D S
X J Y D B T N G W F M Z F W H I O S R V K Q M O O I M C G C
S E V B I B Z N N K I B J T F K B H Q J X E K Y T F Y C B H
H W T V X U A D F Y A E A A E H S B L G Y R E D N Z B Y F A
P U H Z Q U X V C B C O V M N F V R J R J C O N X W F M C R
O J W P U T P T T Q T Z J T B W Y X O R A C Q D P C H W W D
N A Q H N R S L P O K T W V X O P H V L O B R G S X P G G P
G Q S F T S S B L N A W O U H P O J L G P H I L O T O Q H J
B C H E H M J Z S I V W T E F N J K F X A U E Y H B Z F U G
R R E N L W I C K O J V D M G C L H H U Q R M H K W X L L F
V E G N O L E C F N A H F S H J H W E U A D L O S I E W I K
F V X E C O A X K F T Z M U I W I S W P F H L I K C V O B J
F C J L A A G I Z P U G S K I Z R H N V P I K K C D A O I M
Y P E H K J R J B N J J A L R J K N T D D B G F S Z N X U H
V J O S Y R A E A E R H Y I E H L V F F R X F T J Z N H X X
Z B A U X V G U A E A W H B M L A R K J X A H Q D N N B Q T
C K X X S X O K W D C X T H X A B I P Y O P X E F U Q W I A
```

Cauliflower	Bamboo	Kohlrabi	Rhubarb
Shallot	Broccoli	Celery	Fennel
Garlic	Onion	Leek	Fig
Swiss Chard	Asparagus	Lotus Root	

Tip – Learn to Love Vegetables

Broccoli is a very healthy stem vegetable that aids digestion, prevents constipation, maintains low blood sugar, is rich in fiber, and keeps you from overeating.

However, some people just do not like broccoli (and other healthy vegetables). Here are some tips that may help:

- Eat small portions – eat just a few bites at each meal until you just cannot live without it.
- Cut into smaller pieces so that the taste and texture are not overwhelming.
- Mix with something you do like to eat, like mashed potatoes.
- Use seasoning, melted cheese, salsa, ketchup, or other dressing to make it taste yummy to you. (Go light on the extras, though as many are high in calories and salt.)

Image of broccoli and cheese

Leaves

Leaves make food using sunlight through photosynthesis. Leaves are often flat to absorb more sunlight. They absorb carbon dioxide and release oxygen.

Some edible leaves include mint, spinach, kale, greens, and cabbage.

Plants with leaves that remain green all year are called evergreens. Plants that shed their leaves are deciduous and usually lose their autumn leaves. The leaves grow back in spring.

Leaves come in many shapes and sizes. The largest leaves can be found in Borneo and can be ten feet across. There are two primary leaf forms – simple leaf with an undivided form and compound leaf with two or more blades.

Activity – Evergreen Leaves
Look at evergreen leaves. What is different about them?

_____
_____

Activity – Counting Leaves

AN ADDITION GAME

Directions: Count how many of each type leaf you see.
Write the answers in the box provided below.

Simple [   ]   Compound [   ]

Activity – Leaf Tasting

Taste several different edible leaves like lettuce, spinach, mint. Which is your favorite and why?

_____
_____

There are eight (8) compound and seven (7) simple.

Activity – Sort Leaves

Take a walk and collect different types of leaves. Sort them into evergreen and deciduous. Glue them to card stock in two columns like the image below. Which type of leaf is your favorite?

_____
_____

EVERGREENS | DECIDUOUS

Flowers

Flowers generally produce seeds to make new plants.

Examples of edible flowers include pansies, roses, violets, daisies, and nasturtiums.

It must be pollinated for a flower to produce seeds or new life. Some flowers are self-pollinated, which means they can create a new life without another plant or animal. Sunflowers and many kinds of orchids are self-pollinating.

Other flowers need to be cross-pollinated, which means the flower needs pollen from another plant to create seeds. A butterfly or bee will pick up pollen when visiting a flower. Then it will flutter over to another flower, and some of that pollen will land on the new flower. This pollinates the new flower. Squash and pumpkins require cross-pollination.

Image of sunflowers and squash

Activity – Flowers Coloring Page

Edible Flowers

Warning: Before eating any flowers, check with a professional. Not every flower is edible. Some flowers are toxic and can make you very sick.

Never harvest flowers growing by the roadside or in the wild.

Correctly identify the flower and eat only edible flowers and edible parts of those flowers.

Use flowers sparingly in recipes due to digestive issues caused by eating large quantities.

Be aware that individuals may experience allergic reactions.

Here is a list of common flowers that are also edible. (Stradley, n.d.)

Begonia	English Daisy	Pansy
Calendula	Hibiscus	Phlox
Marigold	Honeysuckle	Primrose
Chrysanthemum	Impatiens	Rose
Clover	Lilac	Sunflower
Dandelion	Nasturtium	

Disclaimer: Individuals consuming the flowers listed in this handbook do so entirely at their own risk. Neither the author, publisher, nor Hickory Greenway Harvest can be held responsible for any adverse reaction to the flowers.

Experiment – Edible Flower Popsicles

Warning: We recommend a parent supervise any culinary activities. See the warning on the previous page for more information on edible flowers.

Edible Flower Popsicles

Ingredients:

For the Popsicles:

2 cups Coconut Water

¼ cup Rose Syrup

Edible Flowers

Popsicle Molds & Popsicle Sticks

For the Rose Syrup:

½ cup Sugar

½ cup Water

1 tsp Rosewater

Instructions:

1. Combine sugar and water over medium heat, stirring until the sugar dissolves. Cook for an additional 5 minutes as it simmers. Take off heat and add the rosewater. Cool completely.

2. Stir together the coconut water and syrup. Place 3 to 5 flowers in each popsicle mold and fill with coconut water mixture.

3. Pop in the freezer until your edible flower popsicles are completely frozen. Take the popsicles out of the mold and enjoy!

Fruit

The fruit is usually considered any sweet-tasting plant part. However, a fruit is a protective covering for seeds. A bean pod and a peanut shell are both fruit, while the beans and peanuts are seeds.

Examples of edible fruits are watermelon, pumpkins, squash, tomatoes, cucumbers, olives, oranges, peaches, green beans, and peanuts.

Activity – Name That Fruit

Many fruits are commonly mistaken for vegetables. One example is tomatoes. Tomatoes contain seeds, so they are fruit, but most people think tomatoes are vegetables. How many fruits that are thought to be vegetables can you name?

Tomato	

Image of green beans and cucumbers

Activity – Fruit Math

FRUIT MATH

LET'S ADD THESE FRUITS UP!

Directions: How many fruits can you see?
Add them all up, then write the answer in the box

Activity – Mr. Greene's Fruit Stand

Mr. Greene's Fruit Stand

**Mr. Greene sells fruit in boxes of 7.
Make sure each box has seven by drawing the missing fruit.**

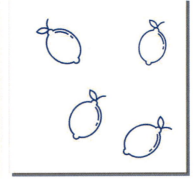

Seeds

A seed is the plant part that can grow into a new plant.

Examples of edible seeds include sunflower seeds, walnuts, peas, beans, and pumpkin seeds.

Seeds come in all sizes and shapes. The mustard seed is among the smallest seeds, and the coconut is one of the largest seeds.

Activity – Look at Those Seeds
As you eat fruit, wash a few seeds of each and collect. When you have ten different types, sort them from smallest to largest. Take a picture of your new collection.

"The kingdom of heaven is like to a grain of mustard seed, which is the smallest of all seeds on earth. Yet when planted, it grows and becomes the largest of all garden plants, with such big branches that the birds can perch in its shade." (Jesus, 30 AD)

Jesus, The Holy Bible

Experiment – See Your Seed Germinate

Using a clear jar, plant a seed next to the glass so it is visible from the outside. Follow the directions that came with the seeds to care for your growing plant. Watch it grow. Record your observations below.

Day 2	No sign of sprouting yet
Day 3	
Day 4	
Day 5	
Day 6	
Day 7	
Day 8	
Day 9	
Day 10	
Day 11	
Day 12	
Day 13	
Day 14	

Image of a bean plant in various stages of growth

Experiment – Can Seeds Sprout Without Soil?

Materials:

- 4 zippered sandwich bags
- 4 paper towels
- 8 bean seeds (any seed should work)
- Sharpie marker to write on the bags

Instructions:

1. Dampen paper towels but do not soak.
2. Place a seed onto each paper towel and fold loosely.
3. Place into a zippered bag and seal.
4. Label bag with the date & seed type.
5. Place the bag(s) into a warm place.
6. Check the paper towels daily and slightly dampen them when they start to dry.
7. You should start to see some sprouting progress within a week. Once the seeds sprout, transfer to a small pot with soil and place in a sunny place.

Record your observations below.

Day 2	No sign of sprouting yet
Day 3	
Day 4	
Day 5	
Day 6	
Day 7	
Day 8	
Day 9	
Day 10	
Day 11	
Day 12	
Day 13	
Day 14	

"*The love of gardening is a seed once sown that never dies.*" (Jekyll, n.d.)

Gertrude Jekyll, British horticulturist

Activity – Plant Parts

Draw a line from the word to the part of the plant that cooresponds.

Activity – Name That Part

NAME THAT PART!

Can you name these plant parts?

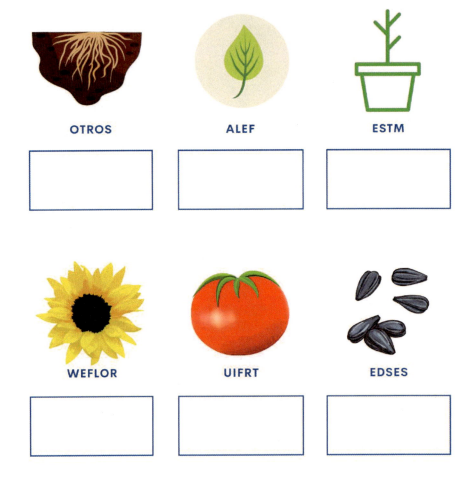

PLANT TYPES

Plant Types

Botanists, or plant scientists, group plants into four main groups – mosses and worts, ferns, gymnosperms, and angiosperms. These plant types either have flowers or no flowers and have a vascular system that allows water to travel through the plant or have no vascular system.

Vascular System

Vascular System

From the roots, up the stem, out the branches, through to the leaf tips, water flows through the plant's vascular system.

Pollinators

Pollinators

Bats, bees, beetles, birds, and butterflies are all plant pollinators - flitting from flower to flower picking up pollen and seeds to help flowering plants reproduce.

Mosses & Worts

Mosses and Worts are non-flowering, non-vascular plants that do not grow very tall.

Mosses
- Grow no taller than one inch in height.
- Need water to reproduce.
- Live in moist areas out of direct sunlight.
- Have a waxy outer covering that helps hold in moisture.

Worts
- Are the simplest form of a plant.
- Do not have roots.
- Have tiny hairs or rhizoids on them.
- Grow in a flat leafy form on the ground.
- Some types of Worts live in water.

Activity – Mosses & Worts
Which is a wort and not a moss? _____

Ferns

Ferns are vascular, non-flowering plants that reproduce by spores.

- They have roots, leaves, stems, and trunks.
- They grow taller than mosses and Worts.
- They need water to reproduce.
- They can live anywhere if there is plenty of moisture.

Gymnosperms

Gymnosperms are non-flowering, vascular plants that reproduce by seeds found in cones.

- Sometimes called conifers.
- Cold climate types include pine and spruce trees.
- Warm climate types include cycads.
- They need the wind to help spread their seeds.

Activity – Gymnosperms

Which one is not a gymnosperm? _____

Angiosperms

Angiosperms are flowering, vascular plants with seeds that grow inside a fruit.

- 80% of all plants are angiosperms.
- They have roots, stems, and leaves.
- Apple trees, grass, and roses are examples of angiosperms.
- Like bees and butterflies, they use pollinators to spread and pollinate their seeds.

Sunflowers are synonymous with adoration, longevity, and loyalty. Like the sun they resemble, sunflowers are known for being "happy" flowers and bring much joy to those who receive them.

Activity – Plant Types Crossword

Crossword Puzzle

Down:
1. tiny hairs
2. plant that grows flowers
3. create new life
4. an angiosperm's seeds grow within this plant part
5. simplest type of plant
6. feathery plant that can grow anywhere with sufficient moisture
10. helps an angiosperm or gymnosperm reproduce
12. can reproduce like a seed
13. low-growing plant that grows out of direct sunlight

Across:
7. available water
8. system through which water flows
9. flowering plant; example - sunflower
11. non-flowering plant; example - pine tree
14. gymnosperm that has seeds growing inside of a cone

Activity – How Seeds Travel

How Seeds Travel

Seeds Travel In Several Ways: A) blown by the wind, B) stuck on animals, or C) eaten/carried by animals. Which way are the following seeds carried?

A, B, B, C, C, A

PLANT LIFE CYCLE TYPES

Plant Life Cycle Types

Before planning your garden, it is essential to know your plants' life cycle. Annual plants will die during the winter season and must be replanted in the spring. Biennial plants are similar to annuals but have a two-year life cycle. Perennials may die back in winter but will grow again in spring. Their life cycle may be three to five years or even longer.

Annuals

Annual plants germinate, flower, set seed, and die in one season. Their goal is to create seeds.

Cool-Season Annuals

These plants are hardy and thrive in cool-to-moderate early spring temperatures and fall, and can tolerate light frost exposure. Calendula, Dianthus, Pansy, Poppy, Primrose, Sweet Pea are cool-season annuals.

Warm-Season Annuals

Warm-season annuals are native to warmer climates and thrive during warmer months. Wait until late spring to plant. Geranium, Impatiens, Marigold, Morning Glory, Sunflower, and Zinnia are warm-season annuals.

The Rest (Half-Hardy)
These plants are most common and tolerate a wide range of temperatures. However, they should be planted after the danger of frost has passed. Begonia, Dahlia, Gazania, and Gerbera are good examples of half-hardy.

Choosing Annuals
Annuals are perfect for filling in bare spots in an established garden or containers. As they mature faster than perennials and often bloom from planting time to frost, they offer beauty all season.

Biennials

Biennial plants will grow to mature size in two years and then die. They usually bloom in their second year.

Beets, Brussels Sprouts, Cabbage, Carrots, and Celery are biennials.

Perennials

Perennial plants are hardier than annuals and usually bloom for only one season a year. These plants vary significantly in care and maintenance. Some need to be pruned and divided regularly to thrive and keep tidy, while others need almost no maintenance. Apple trees, Azalea, Basil, Hosta, Peony, Phlox, and Strawberry, are perennials.

Temperennials

These plants are perennials in warmer climates but act as annuals in colder climates. Elephant Ear, Mangave, Succulents, and Yellow Bell are temperennials.

Choosing Perennials

Although they cost more initially, they will return year after year, require less water once established, and create a home for pollinators and wildlife. If you want a lower maintenance garden, perennials are an excellent choice.

Activity – Perennials

HOW PLANTS GROW

How Plants Grow

Most plants grow from seeds. The seeds from existing plants are blown or carried to new places, where the seeds germinate, sprout, and grow into new plants. These new plants have their seeds that are blown or carried away, and again new plants are created. This is called the plant life cycle and describes how plants reproduce or create new plants.

However, seeds must have the right ingredients to grow – light, water, air, and nutrients. Sunlight, rain, wind, and good soil provide all these necessary ingredients for plants to grow healthy and strong.

Some plants just need a little sunlight, and some grow better in full sun for eight or more hours a day. In the same way, some need a little moisture like a cactus, and some require much water to be healthy, like a Water Lilly. Knowing your plant's needs helps you decide where to place your plant, how often the plant needs to be watered, and what kind of soil your plant requires.

Botanists have been studying plants for a very long time and have determined how much light, water, and nutrients plants need to thrive. If you purchase seeds or a baby plant, the tag or envelope will tell you exactly what your plant needs.

In the example below, the spacing, depth, light, soil temperature, and growing instructions are all listed to make it easy to grow a healthy sunflower.

Plant Life Cycle

LIFE CYCLE OF A SUNFLOWER

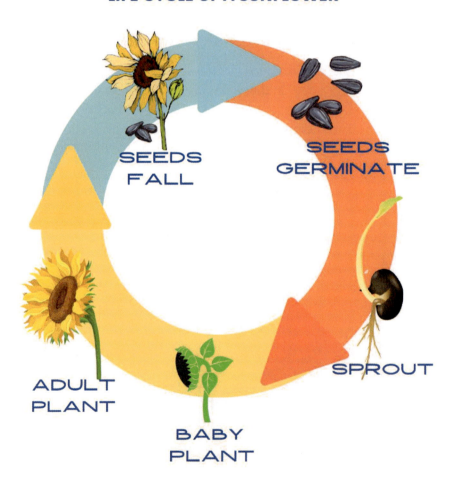

Plant Tags

Plant tags tell you how to grow and maintain your plant successfully. The tag may use words, icons, or a mixture of both to indicate important information. A typical tag will contain information as listed below.

Name

A plant tag will include both the botanical (or scientific) and common name for the plant. For example, a tag for "Bellflowers" (common) will also include "Campanula" (botanical). There are often many varieties of a plant. However, the botanical name will be specific to the plant to which the tag refers.

Description

A brief description of a particular variety and its unique features. May indicate whether the plant is miniature, compact, or otherwise smaller than the usual variety.

Light ☀

Plants will have different light requirements from "I just adore the sun" to "I can't stand the heat." Bellflowers can be planted in a location that gets full sun and in a location that has partial shade.

Full Sun ☀

A plant that prefers full sun requires 6 - 8 hours of direct sunlight a day.

Part Sun ⛅

A plant that prefers part sun requires only 3 - 6 hours of direct sunlight a day.

Full Shade ☁

A plant that prefers full shade cannot tolerate direct sunlight's heat and needs more moisture to thrive.

AFRICAN MARIGOLD
CLAVELON AFRICANO
TAGETES ERECTA

BLOOM SEASON
SPRING, SUMMER, FALL

SUN EXPOSURE
6+ HOURS DIRECT SUN

WATER
2X PER WEEK, MORE OFTEN WHEN DRY

ZONE
ALL ZONES, NON-HARDY BELOW 40° F

SIZE
18-20" H X 10-12" W

SPACING
8-12"

PLANTING STEPS

1. DIG HOLE 2X WIDTH OF POT
2. PLANT 1" ABOVE GROUND LEVEL
3. BUILD WATER BASIN
4. MULCH AND WATER THOROUGHLY

Water

New plants require more moisture more often than established plants. Pay close attention to water requirements and whether the requirements are for new or established plants. Bellflowers require normal or well-drained soil.

Dry or Very Well-Drained
Let the soil dry out between watering.

Normal or Well-Drained
The soil, down to an inch below the surface, should be moist.

Moist or Damp
The soil should stay moist.

Bloom Time

Plants bloom at different times – some bloom all season, some in early spring, and some in fall. Some flowers do not bloom until the second year of growth. Bellflowers bloom in early summer to early fall.

Spacing

Differing plants need to be planted at different distances, both in depth and width. Some plants will die if planted too closely. Others may not grow if the seeds or roots are too deep.

Size

Since differing plants grow to different heights and widths, the size will indicate the mature plant's estimated maximum height and width. Bellflowers grow up to 4' in height.

Shape
Plants have different shapes or "habits." Some creep, some grow straight up, and some grow together in a hedge.

Zone
This information will indicate the zones in which the plant will thrive.

Care
Plants have different maintenance needs. Some need regular pruning, fertilizing, or deadheading, while others prefer to be left alone.

Use
Some plants thrive in containers, some are great borders, while others are great for shade gardens. This section will indicate the plant's best utilization.

Wildlife
Plants can either attract certain types of wildlife or be resistant to certain wildlife types.

Attracts
Some plants attract butterflies, bees, and birds. If planting a pollinator garden, ensure that the plant attracts one or more of these wildlife types.

Detracts
Some plants are resistant to wildlife, like deer and rabbits. Being resistant means that deer and rabbits will not munch on the plant. These types of plants would be suitable to border a vegetable garden.

Planting Steps
Detailed instructions on how to plant.

Keep or Toss
One of the most asked questions is, "Should I keep or toss the plant tags?" Our recommendation is to keep one tag of each variety of plant and list the

location and date planted. Try putting your tags on a key chain to help keep them organized.

Activity – Different Tags

Different seed and plant companies will use different symbols, information, and layouts for their plant tags. If you are unsure which company to buy from, their tag information may just be the deciding factor. The more you know about a plant, the better chance you have that it will thrive in your environment under your educated care.

Peruse the different company tags at a local nursery or hardware store. Which tags do you like best and why?

_____
_____

Seed packets should also have the same information as a plant tag.

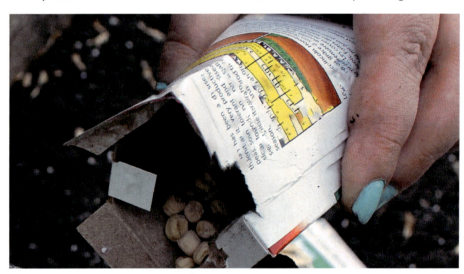

Activity – Color Peony

HOW PLANTS EAT

How Plants Eat

Plants do not eat in the same way that people and animals eat. Instead, they make their food through a process call photosynthesis. In this process, the plant's leaves absorb sunlight and carbon dioxide from the air into tiny chloroplasts within the leaves. When carbon dioxide mixes with light energy and water, it creates a type of sugar through a chemical reaction. This simple sugar is then spread throughout the plant via its vascular system.

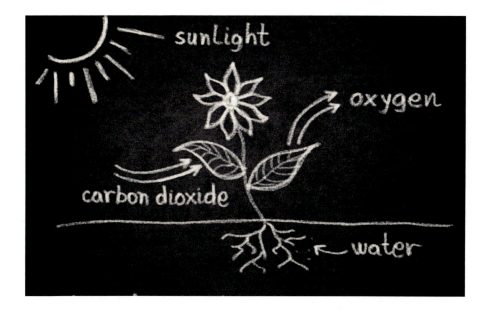

During the process, the plant also releases oxygen back into the air. People and animals breathe in that oxygen and breathe out carbon dioxide. In this way, we have a symbiotic relationship, which is another way of saying that people and animals need plants to live. Furthermore, plants need people and animals to live.

Image showing symbiotic relationship between people and plants

Another image of the photosynthesis process

Chlorophyll

Chlorophyll is the substance (pigment) that gives plants their green color. It helps plants absorb energy and get their nutrients from sunlight during the photosynthesis process. Chlorophyll is found inside the tiny chloroplasts of plant leaves.

Question – Do Plants Bleed?
Plants do not have blood as we do, and therefore, do not bleed. However, if cut, the plant does produce a substance to repair the wound, much like our bodies do.

WHERE PLANTS GROW

Where Plants Grow

Plants grow everywhere. They grow on land, on mountain tops, and in the desert. They grow in oceans, lakes, and rivers. They even grow in the coldest, harshest area – Antarctica. There are plants that are suited to every climate zone and environment in our world.

Zone

The USDA has divided our country into "growing zones" by weather, temperature, and environmental conditions. When considering a particular plant variety, ensure it will grow well in your zone. To find your zone, navigate to https://planthardiness.ars.usda.gov/PHZMWeb/ and view your state map. (USDA, 2012)

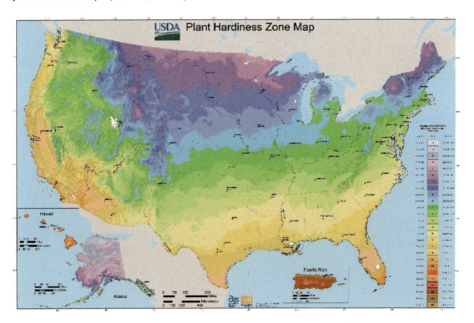

Research – Your Growing Zone
Record your zone below and refer to it each time you consider buying plants or seeds. _____

Native Plants

Plants grow best in their native environment. A plant is considered a native if it originates from a plant that occurs naturally in the same region or environment in which it grows without human intervention, transplant, or introduction. Natives tend to thrive in the soil, moisture, and weather in that region. Carolina Lupine is native to North Carolina – see image below.

Research – Native Plants

Research native plants in your area. Record your top five favorites below.

1	
2	
3	
4	
5	

Soil

Like plants, the soil differs from region to region. There are over four hundred types of soil in North Carolina alone. The three most common soil types are Cecil soil, sandhill soil, and organic wetland soil.

Cecil soil is fertile, well-draining red clay soil, covering over 1.5 million NC acres. This soil type is North Carolina's official state soil and is suited for growing corn, cotton, and tobacco.

Sandhill soil is gray, loose, and sandy soil with low organic matter. Sandhill soil is parched and unsuited for most crops. However, some fruit trees with deep roots, like peach and apple, do well with this soil type.

Organic wetland soil, commonly found in bogs, marshes, and swamps, is usually black and contains high levels of peat or decomposed vegetation. While too wet and mucky to grow crops efficiently, wetland soil is very well suited to many plants.

Image from top to bottom: Cecil, sandhill, and wetland soils

Research – Native Soil

What type of soil do you have in your area? Record the growing characteristics of your soil.

_____
_____

HOW PLANTS MOVE

How Plants Move

Animals and people have ways of moving from place to place. As plants have roots, they cannot move from place to place. However, they can move their plant bodies. There are two types of plant movement – tropic and nastic movement.

Tropic movement is the movement towards or away from a stimulus – light (the sun), water (rain), touch (a bee), gravity, or chemicals (fertilizer or herbicide). Nastic movement is a non-stimulus movement like the closing of a tulip's flower at night.

Activity – Pretend To Be A Flower
Stand in place. Your feet can not move as they are rooted like a flower's roots. Your hands are leaves, your arms and legs are stems, and your head is a flower.

1. Turn slowly toward a light source – the sun, a sunny window, a lamp. Slowly reach your hands towards the light. This is a tropic movement.
2. Pretend it is night. Slowly move your hands towards your body and place each hand on the opposite shoulder. Stand straight and tall and close your eyes. This is a nastic movement.

Image of a ladybug

Activity – Recap Word Search

EXPLORING PLANTS

```
E U Y K D V O P G W G E R M I N A T E Z
N M V P E R E N N I A L B E J R G V P V
H A B B L D E K O O I C K I E P O J I Z
L N Z Y R T A J M D R Y B Z B O X B J O
T N C K T Z R U M Y D I E V R L A I Z N
E U O F A N P O L I F E C Y C L E E P E
M A Q I Z Y G H P F K L Q P M I Y N T R
P L I B T H G D O I I J A Y X N E N B O
E S N R Q F Q C O T C E Q L T A W I E L
R F A O F I P R O H O G X Z X T U A S O
E T S U Q S P R O U T S V A Y O N L T R
N R T S H I Y G I A F U Y A A R F T H N
N G I D D L L X Y Y H X T N N P I I E A
I E C S Z B K H Y V O L B C T X V J C T
A W D J E W D E C I D U O U S H Z U J I
L C C I T E C N B G U C I V H N E Q B V
Z S G E B S D L U W M T F D R T T S B E
V J Z Z R L F S O I L G L Y R P N E I Z
H Z U X P K E N U T R I E N T S L L G S
J G J F B O T A N I S T B G W Z E I K J
```

photosynthesis	temperennial	pollinator	perennial
deciduous	germinate	biennial	nutrients
botanist	fibrous	native	sprout
tropic	annual	edible	life cycle
seeds	soil	nastic	zone

GLOSSARY

Glossary

annual – *noun* a plant that will germinate, flower, set seed, and die in one season. Its goal is to create seeds

biennial – *noun* a plant that will grow to mature size in two years and then die. It will usually bloom in its second year

botanist – *noun* a scientist that studies plants

chlorophyll – *noun* the pigment responsible for a plant's green color

deciduous – *noun* a type of shrub or tree that sheds its leaves annually – usually in the fall

edible – *adj* safe to be eaten

essential – *adj* necessary or critical

evergreens – *noun* a plant that retains green leaves all year. Pine trees are a type of evergreen

fertilizer – *noun* manure or a mixture of nitrates used to make the soil more fertile

fibrous root system – *noun* a root system that contains or looks like fibers. Grasses are a type of fibrous root system

flower – *noun* the seed-bearing part of the plant. An example would be the daisy

fruit – *noun* the sweet product of the tree, shrub, or other plant containing seeds. Examples include mangoes and papaya

germinate – *verb* to grow or sprout

germination – *noun* the process whereby seeds sprout and begin to grow

internode – *noun* the part of the plant stem between nodes

leaf – *noun* a flat (usually oval) part of the plant attached to the stem that uses photosynthesis to make food for the plant

> **compound leaf** – *noun* a leaf divided, forming two or more distinct blades. Walnut trees have compound leaves

> **simple leaf** – *noun* a leaf that is undivided and has a single blade

life cycle – *noun* the process by which seeds germinate, sprout, grow into mature plants, release seeds, and die

nastic – *noun* non-stimulus plant movement like the closing of a tulip's flower at night

native – *noun* a seed or plant that naturally originates in the same region or environment in which it grows, without human intervention, transplant, or introduction. Native seeds tend to thrive in the soil, moisture, and weather in that region

node – *noun* the part of the plant stem from which one or more leaves emerge, often forming a small knob

nutrients – *noun* a substance that provides nourishment vital for growth and the maintenance of life

perennial – *noun* a plant that costs more initially, will return year after year, require less water once established, and create a home for pollinators and wildlife

photosynthesis – *noun* the process by which plants use sunlight to make food

pollination – *noun* the transfer of pollen to a flower to allow fertilization

> **cross-pollination** – *noun* the pollination of a plant with pollen from another flower or plant

> **self-pollination** – *noun* pollination of a flower from the same flower's pollen or by pollen of another flower on the same plant

pollinator – *noun* anything that carries pollen from the male to the female part of the same or another flower. Birds, bees, and butterflies are pollinators

root – *noun* the plant part that attaches the plant to the ground for support and moves water and nutrients up to the stem and leaves

seed – *noun* the part of the plant that can develop into a new plant

soil – *noun* the upper layer of dirt in which plants grow

sprout – *verb* to grow shoots

stem – *noun* the plant's central part or stalk that supports the leaves, flowers, and fruit and moves water and nutrients

taproot root system – *noun* a root system with a central root and small roots or fibers attached

temperennial – *noun* a plant that acts as a perennial in warmer climates and as an annual in colder climates

tropic – *noun* plant movement towards or away from a stimulus – light, water, touch, gravity, or chemicals

vegetable – *noun* a part of a plant used as food – examples include potato, carrot, or asparagus

Research – Add Your Definitions

List other words that you have learned and their meaning:

Word	Meaning

RESOURCES

Resources

Certificate of Completion

Once you have completed this workbook, you may take an online exam at www.juniorgardeningexplorers.com/exams to receive a certificate of completion. You may also receive a free promotional gift while supplies last.

Citations

Jekyll, G. (n.d.). *Gertrude Jekyll*. Retrieved from Brainy Quote: https://www.brainyquote.com/quotes/gertrude_jekyll_310275

Jesus. (30 AD). The Holy Bible. In Jesus, *The Holy Bible* (p. MATTHEW 13:31 KJV).

Stradley, L. (n.d.). *Edible Flowers*. Retrieved from What's Cooking America: https://whatscookingamerica.net/EdibleFlowers/EdibleFlowersMain.htm

USDA. (2012). *USDA Plant Hardiness Zone Map*. Retrieved from USDA: https://planthardiness.ars.usda.gov/PHZMWeb/

Answers

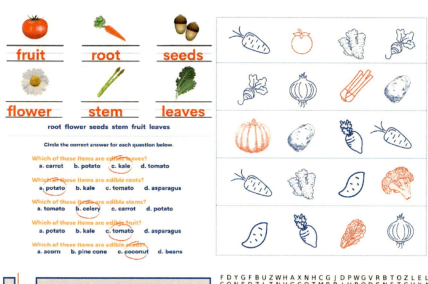

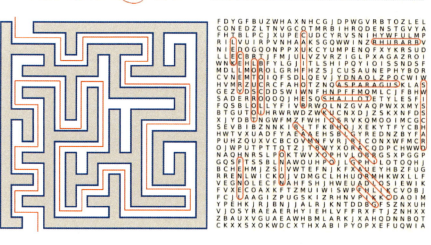

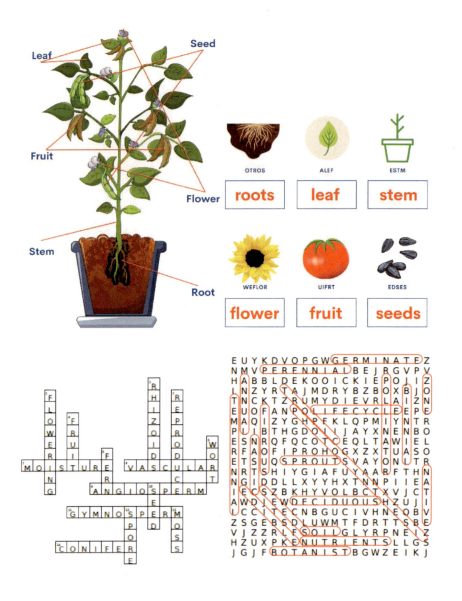

Notes

A Note from the Author

I am the grandmother of four precious children, a Master Gardener, and a Hickory Greenway Harvest Inc (HGH) board member. Like HGH, I believe it is essential to teach gardening skills to the next generations and to bring back the traditions that sustained us in the past. Everyone needs access to good, healthy, local foods.

HGH's mission statement:

"We work to facilitate a cooperative effort of multiple organizations in order to provide fresh grown produce and feed the less fortunate of our community; to provide educational opportunities that demonstrate the art of cultivating the land for agricultural use, and to develop a grassroots campaign that brings the community together to foster sustainable support for our fellow citizens."

Check out HGH's website at www.hickorygreenwayharvest.org for more information.

If you have enjoyed this workbook, check out our other workbooks and our Junior Gardening Explorers "Crew" at www.juniorgardeningexplorers.com.

Michele S Long, Author *Morgan Long Photography, NC*